PROMISES&
PRAYERS

FOR TIMES OF
UNCERTAINTY

The quoted ideas expressed in this book (but not Scripture verses) are not, in all cases, exact quotations, as some have been edited for clarity and brevity. In all cases, the author has attempted to maintain the speaker's original intent. In some cases, quoted material for this book was obtained from secondary sources, primarily print media. While every effort was made to ensure the accuracy of these sources, the accuracy cannot be guaranteed. For additions, deletions, corrections, or clarifications in future editions of this text, please write Freeman-Smith, LLC.

The Holy Bible, King James Version

The Holy Bible, New King James Version (NKJV) Copyright © 1982 by Thomas Nelson, Inc. Used by permission.

New Century Version®. (NCV) Copyright © 1987, 1988, 1991 by Word Publishing, a division of Thomas Nelson, Inc. All rights reserved. Used by permission.

The Holman Christian Standard Bible™ (Holman CSB) Copyright © 1999, 2000, 2001 by Holman Bible Publishers. Used by permission.

The Holy Bible, New International Version®. (NIV) Copyright © 1973, 1978, 1984 International Bible Society. Used by permission of Zondervan. All rights reserved.

The Holy Bible. New Living Translation (NLT) copyright © 1996 Tyndale Charitable Trust. Used by permission of Tyndale House Publishers.

Scripture taken from The Message. (MSG) Copyright © 1993, 1994, 1995, 1996, 2000, 2001, 2002. Used by permission of NavPress Publishing Group.

Cover Design by Kim Russell/Wahoo Designs
Page Layout by Bart Dawson

ISBN 978-1-60587-047-2

Printed in the United States of America

31 daily devotions

PROMISES& PRAYERS

FOR TIMES OF
UNCERTAINTY

TABLE OF CONTENTS

INTRODUCTION

*"We know that all things work together
for the good of those who love God:
those who are called according to His purpose."*

Romans 8:28 Holman CSB

God's Word promises that all things work together for the good of those who love Him. Yet sometimes we encounter situations that seem so troubling that we simply cannot comprehend how these events might be a part of God's plan for our lives. We experience tough times—perhaps the loss of money or health; perhaps divorce, job loss, or a broken personal relationship. The future seems uncertain, and we honestly wonder if recovery is possible. But with God, all things are possible.

The Christian faith, as communicated through the words of the Holy Bible, is a healing faith. It offers comfort in times of trouble, courage for our fears, hope instead of hopelessness, certainty not doubt. Through the healing words of God's promises, Christians understand that the Lord continues to manifest His plan in good times and hard times.

If you are experiencing the pain of a recent setback, or if you are worried about the vagaries of an uncertain future, this book is intended to help. So, during the next 31 days, try this experiment: read one chapter a day and take the ideas in that chapter to heart. Then, apply those lessons to the everyday realities of your life. When you weave God's message into the fabric of your day, you'll quickly discover that God's Word has the power to change everything, including you.

Adversity is not meant to be feared, it is meant to be worked through. If this text assists you, even in a small way, as you move through and beyond your own time of uncertainty, it will have served its purpose. May God bless you and keep you, and may He place His hand upon your heart today and forever.

Day 1

GOD'S PROMISES FOR YOUR UNCERTAIN TIMES

Cast your burden on the Lord,
and He will support you;
He will never allow the righteous to be shaken.
Psalm 55:22 Holman CSB

Never be afraid to trust an unknown future
to a known God.
Corrie ten Boom

These are times of great uncertainty. As we become accustomed to, and at times almost numbed by, a steady stream of unsettling news, we are reminded that our world is in a state of constant change. But God is not. So when the world seems to be trembling beneath our feet, we can be comforted in the knowledge that our Heavenly Father is the rock that cannot be shaken.

Every day that we live, we mortals encounter a multitude of changes—some good, some not so good. And on occasion, all of us must endure life-changing personal losses that leave us heartbroken. When we do, our Heavenly Father stands ready to comfort us, to guide us, and—in time—to heal us.

Is the world spinning a little too fast for your liking? Are you facing troubling uncertainties, difficult circumstances, or unwelcome changes? If so, please remember that God is far bigger than any problem you may face. So, instead of worrying about life's inevitable challenges, put your faith in the Father and His only begotten Son. After all, "Jesus Christ is the same yesterday, today, and forever" (Hebrews 13:8 NKJV). And it is precisely because your Savior does not change that you can face your challenges with courage for today and hope for tomorrow.

Are you anxious about situations that you cannot control? Take your anxieties to God. Are you troubled? Take your troubles to Him. Does your little corner of the universe seem to be a frightening place? Seek protection from the One who cannot be moved. The same God who created the universe will protect you if you ask Him . . . so ask Him . . . and then serve Him with willing hands and a trusting heart.

TODAY'S TIP FOR HANDLING TOUGH TIMES

As you face uncertain times, make sure to build your future on a firm foundation: the unshakable foundation of God's eternal promises.

MORE FROM GOD'S WORD ABOUT
CHANGING TIMES

I the Lord do not change.

Malachi 3:6 Holman CSB

The sensible see danger and take cover; the foolish keep going and are punished.

Proverbs 27:12 Holman CSB

But may the God of all grace, who called us to His eternal glory by Christ Jesus, after you have suffered a while, perfect, establish, strengthen, and settle you.

1 Peter 5:10 NKJV

Therefore we do not lose heart. Even though our outward man is perishing, yet the inward man is being renewed day by day.

2 Corinthians 4:16 NKJV

Create in me a clean heart, O God, and renew a steadfast spirit within me.

Psalm 51:10 NKJV

QUESTIONS TO CONSIDER

As I think about these uncertain times, am I willing to make God a full partner in my future, or am I trying to carry today's burdens by myself?

_____

_____

Am I willing to spend time every morning with God in prayer and meditation?

_____

_____

Do I trust that God has a glorious plan for my life, even if I cannot understand that plan right now?

_____

_____

A PRAYER FOR TODAY

Dear Lord, because of You, I can face the uncertainties of life with courage, with hope, with wisdom, and with faith. So today and every day, Father, I will study Your Word; I will trust Your promises; and I will follow Your Son. Amen

Day 2

GOD'S PLAN AND YOUR UNCERTAIN TIMES

"For I know the plans I have for you"
—[this is] the Lord's declaration—
"plans for [your] welfare, not for disaster,
to give you a future and a hope."
Jeremiah 29:11 Holman CSB

When terrible things happen, there are
two choices, and only two: We can trust God,
or we can defy Him. We believe that God is
God, He's still got the whole world in His hands
and knows exactly what He's doing, or we must
believe that He is not God and that we are
at the awful mercy of mere chance.
Elisabeth Elliot

I t's an age-old riddle: Why does God allow us to endure times of uncertainty and pain? After all, since we trust that God is all-powerful, and since we trust that His hand shapes our lives, why doesn't He simply rescue us—and our loved ones—from all hardship and pain?

God's Word teaches us again and again that He loves us and wants the best for us. And the Bible also teaches us that God is ever-present and always watchful. So why, we wonder, if God is really so concerned with every detail of our lives, does He permit us to endure emotions like grief, sadness, shame, or fear? And why does He allow tragic circumstances to invade the lives of good people? These questions perplex us, especially when times are tough.

On occasion, all of us face adversity, and throughout life, we all must endure life-changing personal losses that leave us breathless. When we pass through the dark valleys of life, we often ask, "Why me?" Sometimes the answer is obvious—we make mistakes, and we must pay for them. But on other occasions, when we have done nothing wrong, we wonder why God allows us to suffer.

Even when we cannot understand God's plans, we must trust them. And even when we are impatient for our situations to improve, we must trust God's timing. If we seek to live in accordance with His plan for our lives, we must continue to study His Word (in good times and bad), and we must be watchful for His signs, knowing that in time, He will lead us through the valleys, onward to the mountaintop.

FINDING NEW MEANING

Perhaps tough times have turned your world upside down. Maybe it seems to you as if everything in your life has been rearranged. Or perhaps your relationships and your responsibilities have been permanently altered. If so, you may come face to face with the daunting task of finding new purpose for your life. And God is willing to help.

God has an important plan for your life, and part of His plan may well be related to the tough times you're experiencing. After all, you've learned important, albeit hard earned, lessons. And you're certainly wiser today than you were yesterday. So your suffering carries with it great potential: the potential for intense personal growth and the potential to help others.

As you begin to reorganize your life, look for ways to use your experiences for the betterment of others. When you do, you can rest assured that the course of your recovery will depend upon how quickly you discover new people to help and new reasons to live. And as you move through and beyond your own particular tough times, be mindful of this fact: As a survivor, you will have countless opportunities to serve others. By serving others, you will bring glory to God and meaning to the hardships you've endured.

TODAY'S TIP FOR HANDLING TOUGH TIMES

Sometimes, waiting faithfully for God's plan to unfold is more important than understanding God's plan. Ruth Bell Graham once said, "When I am dealing with an all-powerful, all-knowing God, I, as a mere mortal, must offer my petitions not only with persistence, but also with patience. Someday I'll know why." So even when you can't understand God's plans, you must trust Him and never lose faith!

QUESTIONS TO CONSIDER

Am I really seeking God's will for my life, or am I just going through the motions?

_____

_____

Since I believe that God has a plan for my life, do I believe that He can help me overcome tough times and bring something good out of my hardships?

_____

_____

Do I regularly ask God to reveal His plans to me, and when I pray, do I listen carefully for His response?

_____

_____

A PRAYER FOR TODAY

Dear Lord, even when I am discouraged or when my heart is heavy, I will earnestly seek Your will for my life. You have a plan for me that I can never fully understand. And I will always trust in You. Amen

Day 3

IN TIMES OF ADVERSITY

When you pass through the waters,
I will be with you; and through the rivers,
they shall not overflow you. When you walk through
the fire, you shall not be burned, nor shall the flame
scorch you. For I am the Lord your God,
The Holy One of Israel, your Savior.

Isaiah 43:2-3 NKJV

Troubles we bear trustfully can bring us
a fresh vision of God and a new outlook on life,
an outlook of peace and hope.

Billy Graham

As life here on earth unfolds, all of us encounter occasional disappointments and setbacks: Those occasional visits from Old Man Trouble are simply a fact of life, and none of us are exempt. When tough times arrive, we may be forced to rearrange our plans and our priorities. But even on our darkest days, we must remember that God's love remains constant.

The fact that we encounter adversity is not nearly so important as the way we choose to deal with it. When tough times arrive, we have a clear choice: we can begin the difficult work of tackling our troubles . . . or not. When we summon the courage to look Old Man Trouble squarely in the eye, he usually blinks. But, if we refuse to address our problems, even the smallest annoyances have a way of growing into king-sized catastrophes.

As believers, we know that God loves us and that He will protect us. In times of hardship, He will comfort us; in times of sorrow, He will dry our tears. When we are troubled or weak or sorrowful, God is always with us. We must build our lives on the rock that cannot be shaken: we must trust in God. And then, we must get on with the hard work of tackling our problems . . . because if we don't, who will? Or should?

When Your Faith Is Tested

Life is a mix of good days and difficult days, with good days predominating. During the good days, we are tempted to take our blessings for granted (a temptation that we must resist with all our might). But, during life's difficult days, we discover precisely what we're made of. And more importantly, we discover what our faith is made of.

Has your faith been put to the test yet? If so, then you know that with God's help, you can endure life's darker days. But if you have not yet faced the inevitable trials and tragedies of life, don't worry: you will. And when your faith is put to the test, rest assured that God is perfectly willing—and always ready—to give you strength for the struggle.

Today's Tip for Handling Tough Times

If you're having tough times, don't hit the panic button and don't keep everything bottled up inside. Find a person you can really trust, and talk things over.

More Powerful Ideas About Adversity

The sermon of your life in tough times ministers to people more powerfully than the most eloquent speaker.

Bill Bright

When problems threaten to engulf us, we must do what believers have always done, turn to the Lord for encouragement and solace. As Psalm 46:1 states, "God is our refuge and strength, an ever-present help in trouble."

Shirley Dobson

When we face an impossible situation, all self-reliance and self-confidence must melt away; we must be totally dependent on Him for the resources.

Anne Graham Lotz

If things are tough, remember that every flower that ever bloomed had to go through a whole lot of dirt to get there.

Barbara Johnson

QUESTIONS TO CONSIDER

When tough times arrive, am I willing to place my future in God's hands?

_____

_____

Am I willing to work hard to resolve my own problems, or do I expect other people to solve them for me?

_____

_____

When I face adversity, am I willing to talk things over with family, with trusted friends, and with God . . . or do I keep everything bottled up inside?

_____

_____

A PRAYER FOR TODAY

Lord, when I face disappointments in life, give me perspective and strength to trust Your promises and follow Your will. Then, when I have done my best, let me live with the assurance that You are firmly in control, and that Your love endures forever. Amen

Day 4

FAITH MOVES MOUNTAINS

*For whatever is born of God overcomes the world.
And this is the victory that has
overcome the world—our faith.*

1 John 5:4 NKJV

Trials are not enemies of faith but opportunities
to reveal God's faithfulness.

Barbara Johnson

E very life—including yours—is a grand adventure made great by faith. Every step of the way, through every triumph and tragedy, God will stand by your side and strengthen you . . . if you have faith in Him.

Job had every opportunity to give up on himself and to give up on God. But despite his suffering, Job refused to curse His Creator. Job trusted God in the darkest moments of his life, and so did Jesus.

Before His crucifixion, Jesus went to the Mount of Olives and poured out His heart to God (Luke 22). Jesus knew of the agony that He was destined to endure, but He also knew that God's will must be done. We, like our Savior, face trials that bring fear and trembling to the very depths of our souls, but like Jesus, we should seek God's will, not our own.

When you entrust your life to God completely and without reservation, He will give you the strength to meet life's challenges, the courage to face life's uncertainties, and the wisdom to live in His righteousness and in His peace. So strengthen your faith through praise, through worship, through Bible study, and through prayer. And trust God's plans. With Him, all things are possible, and He

stands ready to open a world of possibilities to you
. . . if you have faith.

Nourish Your faith

When we trust God, we should trust Him
without reservation. But sometimes, especially
during life's darker days, trusting God may be
difficult. Yet this much is certain: whatever our
circumstances, we must continue to plant the
seeds of faith in our hearts, trusting that in time
God will bring forth a bountiful harvest. Planting
the seeds for that harvest requires work, which is
perfectly okay with God. After all, He never gives
us burdens that we cannot bear.

It is important to remember that the work
required to build and sustain our faith is an ongoing
process. Corrie ten Boom advised, "Be filled with
the Holy Spirit; join a church where the members
believe the Bible and know the Lord; seek the
fellowship of other Christians; learn and be
nourished by God's Word and His many promises.
Conversion is not the end of your journey—it is
only the beginning."

The work of nourishing your faith can and
should be joyful work. The hours that you invest

in Bible study, prayer, meditation, and worship should be times of enrichment and celebration. And, as you continue to build your life upon a foundation of faith, you will discover that the journey toward spiritual maturity lasts a lifetime. As a child of God, you are never fully "grown": instead, you can continue "growing up" every day of your life. And that's exactly what God wants you to do.

TODAY'S TIP FOR HANDLING TOUGH TIMES

Feelings come and feelings go, but God never changes. So when you have a choice between trusting your feelings or trusting God, trust God. And remember that if your faith is strong enough, you and God—working together—can move mountains.

QUESTIONS TO CONSIDER

Am I willing to ask God to become a full partner in my life?

_____

_____

Am I willing to pray as if everything depended upon God and work as if everything depended upon me?

_____

_____

After I've done my best, am I willing to trust God's plan and His timetable for my life?

_____

_____

A PRAYER FOR TODAY

Lord, sometimes this world is a terrifying place. When I am filled with uncertainty and doubt, give me faith. In life's dark moments, help me remember that You are always near and that You can overcome any challenge. Today, Lord, and forever, I will place my trust in You. Amen

Day 5

TOUGH
TIMES BUILD
CHARACTER

*The one who lives with integrity lives securely,
but whoever perverts his ways will be found out.*

Proverbs 10:9 Holman CSB

Character is both developed and revealed
by tests, and all of life is a test.

Rick Warren

Psalm 145 promises, "The Lord is near to all who call on him, to all who call on him in truth. He fulfills the desires of those who fear him; he hears their cry and saves them" (vv. 18-20 NIV). And the words of Jesus offer us comfort: "These things I have spoken to you, that in Me you may have peace. In the world you will have tribulation; but be of good cheer, I have overcome the world" (John 16:33 NKJV).

The times that try your soul are also the times that build your character. During the darker days of life, you can learn lessons that are impossible to learn during sunny, happier days. Times of adversity can—and should—be times of intense spiritual and personal growth. But God will not force you to learn the lessons of adversity. You must learn them for yourself.

DO THE HARD THING FIRST

The habit of putting things off until the last minute, along with its first cousin, the habit of making excuses for work that was never done, can be detrimental to your life and to your character.

Are you in the habit of doing what needs to be done when it needs to be done, or are you a dues-paying member of the Procrastinator's Club? If you've acquired the habit of doing things sooner rather than later, congratulations! But, if you find yourself putting off all those unpleasant tasks until later (or never), it's time to think about the consequences of your behavior.

One way that you can learn to defeat procrastination is by paying less attention to your fears and more attention to your responsibilities. So, when you're faced with a difficult choice or an unpleasant responsibility, don't spend endless hours fretting over your fate. Simply seek God's counsel and get busy. When you do, you will be richly rewarded for your willingness to act.

TODAY'S TIP FOR HANDLING TOUGH TIMES

Perhaps, because of tough times, you're being forced to step outside your comfort zone. If so, consider it an opportunity to grow spiritually and emotionally. Your challenge is to believe in yourself, to trust God, and to follow God's lead, even if He leads you outside your comfort zone.

More from God's Word About Character

As the water reflects the face, so the heart reflects the person.

Proverbs 27:19 Holman CSB

We also rejoice in our afflictions, because we know that affliction produces endurance, endurance produces proven character, and proven character produces hope.

Romans 5:3-4 Holman CSB

A good name is to be chosen rather than great riches, loving favor rather than silver and gold.

Proverbs 22:1 NKJV

Do not be deceived: "Evil company corrupts good habits."

1 Corinthians 15:33 NKJV

In all things showing yourself to be a pattern of good works; in doctrine showing integrity, reverence, incorruptibility . . . .

Titus 2:7 NKJV

QUESTIONS TO CONSIDER

Do I believe that tough times can build (or can reveal) character?

_____

_____

Am I determined to learn the lessons that tough times have to teach?

_____

_____

Even when times are tough, do I refuse to compromise my character?

_____

_____

A PRAYER FOR TODAY

Dear Lord, every day can be an exercise in character-building, and that's what I intend to make this day. I will be mindful that my thoughts and actions have great consequences in my own life and in the lives of my loved ones. I will strive to make my thoughts and actions pleasing to You, so that I may be an instrument of Your peace, today and every day. Amen

Day 6

THE LESSONS OF ADVERSITY

He heals the brokenhearted and binds up their wounds.

Psalm 147:3 Holman CSB

God's curriculum for all who sincerely want
to know Him and do His will always includes
lessons
we wish we could skip. With an intimate
understanding of our deepest needs and
individual capacities,
He chooses our curriculum.

Elisabeth Elliot

Whether you're twenty-two or a hundred and two, you've still got lots to learn. Even if you're very wise, God isn't finished with you yet, and He isn't finished teaching you important lessons about life here on earth and life eternal.

God does not intend for you to remain stuck in one place. Far from it! God wants you to continue growing as a person and as a Christian every day that you live. And make no mistake: both spiritual and intellectual growth are possible during every stage of life—during the happiest days or the hardest ones.

How can you make sure that you'll keep growing (and learning) during good times and hard times? You do so through prayer, through worship, through fellowship, through an openness to God's Holy Spirit, and through a careful study of God's Holy Word.

Your Bible contains powerful prescriptions for times of uncertainty. When you study God's Word and live according to His commandments, adversity becomes a practical instructor. While you're enduring difficult days, you learn lessons you simply could not have learned any other way. And when you learn those lessons, you will serve as a shining example to your friends, to you family, and to the world.

OLD MAN TROUBLE HAS LESSONS TO TEACH

The next time Old Man Trouble knocks on your door, remember that he has lessons to teach. So turn away Mr. Trouble as quickly as you can, but as you're doing so, don't forget to learn his lessons. And remember: the trouble with trouble isn't just the trouble it causes; it's also the trouble we cause ourselves if we ignore the things that trouble has to teach. Got that? Then please don't forget it!

Wisdom is the principal thing;
therefore get wisdom.
And in all your getting,
get understanding.

—

Proverbs 4:7 NKJV

MORE POWERFUL IDEAS ABOUT WISDOM

God allows us to experience the low points of life in order to teach us lessons that we could learn in no other way.

C. S. Lewis

What lessons about honor did you learn from your childhood? Are you living what you learned today?

Dennis Swanberg

If your every human plan and calculation has miscarried, if, one by one, human props have been knocked out, take heart. God is trying to get a message through to you, and the message is: "Stop depending on inadequate human resources. Let me handle the matter."

Catherine Marshall

Life is literally filled with God-appointed storms. These squalls surge across everyone's horizon. We all need them.

Charles Swindoll

QUESTIONS TO CONSIDER

Do I understand the importance of seeking God's wisdom and His guidance?

_____

_____

Do I allow God to guide me by His word and by His Spirit?

_____

_____

Do I understand that God still has important lessons to teach me?

_____

_____

A PRAYER FOR TODAY

Dear Lord, sometimes life is so difficult that I can't see any hope for the future. But with You, there is always hope. Keep me mindful that there is nothing that will happen today that You and I can't handle together. Amen

Day 7

IN UNCERTAIN TIMES, GOD TEACHES AND LEADS

Leave inexperience behind, and you will live;
pursue the way of understanding.

Proverbs 9:6 Holman CSB

Your greatest ministry will likely
come out of your greatest hurt.

Rick Warren

From time to time, all of us encounter circumstances that test our faith. When we encounter life's inevitable tragedies, trials, disappointments, and uncertainties we may be tempted to blame God or to rebel against Him. But the Bible reminds us that the trials of life can and should be viewed as tools through which we become "mature and complete, lacking nothing."

Have you recently encountered one of life's inevitable tests? If so, remember that God still has lessons that He intends to teach you. So ask yourself this: what lesson is God trying to teach me today?

TODAY'S TIP FOR HANDLING TOUGH TIMES

Times of change can be times of growth. Elisabeth Elliot reminds us that tough times can lead to a renewal of spirit: "If the leaves had not been let go to fall and wither, if the tree had not consented to be a skeleton for many months, there would be no new life rising, no bud, no flower, no fruit, no seed, no new generation."

WHERE IS GOD LEADING?

Whether we realize it or not, times of uncertainty and adversity can also be times of intense personal and spiritual growth. Our difficult days are also times when we can learn and relearn some of life's most important lessons.

The next time you experience a difficult moment, a difficult day, or a difficult year, ask yourself this question: Where is God leading me? In times of struggle and sorrow, you can be certain that God is leading you to a place of His choosing. Your duty is to watch, to pray, to listen, and to follow.

But grow in the grace and knowledge
of our Lord and Savior Jesus Christ.
To Him be the glory both now
and to the day of eternity.

—

2 Peter 3:18 Holman CSB

QUESTIONS TO CONSIDER

Do I believe that God has lessons to teach me?

_____

_____

Do I believe that I still have "room to grow" in my faith?

_____

_____

Do I believe that spiritual growth usually happens day by day, and do I try to keep growing every day?

_____

_____

A PRAYER FOR TODAY

Dear Lord, when I open myself to You, I am blessed. Let me accept Your love and Your wisdom, Father. Show me Your way, and deliver me from the painful mistakes that I make when I stray from Your commandments. Let me live according to Your Word, and let me grow in my faith every day that I live. Amen

Day 8

No Problems Are Too Big for God

Is anything too hard for the LORD?

Genesis 18:14 KJV

The grace of God is sufficient for all our needs,
for every problem and for every difficulty,
for every broken heart,
and for every human sorrow.

Peter Marshall

Here's a riddle: What is it that is too un-important to pray about yet too big for God to handle? The answer, of course, is: "nothing." Yet sometimes, when the challenges of the day seem overwhelming, we may spend more time worrying about our troubles than praying about them. And, we may spend more time fret-ting about our problems than solving them. A far better strategy, of course, is to pray as if everything depended entirely upon God and to work as if ev-erything depended entirely upon us.

Life is an exercise in problem-solving. The question is not whether we will encounter prob-lems; the real question is how we will choose to address them. When it comes to solving the prob-lems of everyday living, we often know precisely what needs to be done, but we may be slow in doing it—especially if what needs to be done is difficult or uncomfortable for us. So we put off till tomorrow what should be done today.

The words of Psalm 34 remind us that the Lord solves problems for "people who do what is right." And usually, "doing what is right" means doing the uncomfortable work of confronting our problems sooner rather than later. So with no further ado, let the problem-solving begin . . . now!

Do Something Today

Perhaps your troubles are simply too big to solve in a single sitting. But just because you can't solve everything doesn't mean that you should do nothing. So today, as a favor to yourself and as a way of breaking the bonds of procrastination, do something to make your situation better. Even a small step in the right direction is still a step in the right direction. And a small step is far, far better than no step at all.

Today's Tip for Handling Tough Times

Problem-solving 101: When it comes to solving problems, work beats worry. Remember: It is better to fix than to fret.

More Powerful Ideas About Problems

Trial and triumph are what God uses to scribble all over the pages of our lives. They are signs that He is using us, loving us, shaping us to His image, enjoying our companionship, delivering us from evil, and writing eternity into our hearts.

Barbara Johnson

Measure the size of the obstacles against the size of God.

Beth Moore

We must face today as children of tomorrow. We must meet the uncertainties of this world with the certainty of the world to come. To the pure in heart nothing really bad can happen . . . not death, but sin, should be our greatest fear.

A. W. Tozer

Many men owe the grandeur of their lives to their tremendous difficulties.

C. H. Spurgeon

QUESTIONS TO CONSIDER

When I encounter difficulties, do I understand the importance of looking for solutions?

_____

_____

Have I formed the habit of tackling problems sooner rather than later?

_____

_____

When I encounter difficulties, do I work to solve the problems instead of worrying about them, or do I often worry more than I work?

_____

_____

A PRAYER FOR TODAY

Lord, sometimes my problems are simply too big for me, but they are never too big for You. Let me turn my troubles over to You, Lord, and let me trust in You today and for all eternity. Amen

Day 9

THE RIGHT KIND OF ATTITUDE

For God has not given us a spirit of fearfulness,
but one of power, love, and sound judgment.
2 Timothy 1:7 Holman CSB

We are either the masters or the victims of our
attitudes. It is a matter of personal choice.
Who we are today is the result of choices we
made yesterday. Tomorrow, we will become
what we choose today. To change means to
choose to change.

John Maxwell

If you want to defeat Old Man Trouble, you'll need the right kind of attitude: the positive kind. So what's your attitude today? Are you fearful, angry, bored, or worried? Are you pessimistic, perplexed, pained, and perturbed? Are you moping around with a frown on your face that's almost as big as the one in your heart? If so, God wants to have a little talk with you.

God created you in His own image, and He wants you to experience joy, contentment, peace, and abundance. But, God will not force you to experience these things; you must claim them for yourself.

God has given you free will, including the ability to influence the direction and the tone of your thoughts. And, here's how God wants you to direct those thoughts:

"Finally brothers, whatever is true, whatever is honorable, whatever is just, whatever is pure, whatever is lovely, whatever is commendable—if there is any moral excellence and if there is any praise—dwell on these things" (Philippians 4:8 Holman CSB).

The quality of your attitude will help determine the quality of your life, so you must guard your thoughts accordingly. If you make up your mind to approach life with a healthy mixture of realism and optimism, you'll be rewarded. But, if you allow yourself to fall into the unfortunate habit of negative thinking, you will doom yourself to unhappiness or mediocrity, or worse.

So, the next time you find yourself dwelling upon the negative aspects of your life, refocus your attention on things positive. The next time you find yourself falling prey to the blight of pessimism, stop yourself and turn your thoughts around. The next time you're tempted to waste valuable time gossiping or complaining, resist those temptations with all your might.

And remember: You'll never whine your way to the top . . . so don't waste your breath.

TODAY'S TIP FOR HANDLING TOUGH TIMES

A positive attitude leads to positive results; a negative attitude leads elsewhere. And if you want to improve the quality of your thoughts, ask God to help you.

More from God's Word About Attitude

Set your mind on things above, not on things on the earth.

Colossians 3:2 NKJV

Come near to God, and God will come near to you. You sinners, clean sin out of your lives. You who are trying to follow God and the world at the same time, make your thinking pure.

James 4:8 NCV

Those who are pure in their thinking are happy, because they will be with God.

Matthew 5:8 NCV

Finally, brethren, whatever is true, whatever is honorable, whatever is right, whatever is pure, whatever is lovely, whatever is of good repute, if there is any excellence and if anything worthy of praise, dwell on these things.

Philippians 4:8 NASB

So prepare your minds for service and have self-control.

1 Peter 1:13 NCV

QUESTIONS TO CONSIDER

Do I associate with people who are upbeat, optimistic, and encouraging?

_____

_____

Do I try to focus more on my blessings and less on my hardships?

_____

_____

Have I trained myself to look for possibilities, not obstacles?

_____

_____

A PRAYER FOR TODAY

Lord, I pray for an attitude that is Christlike. Whatever my circumstances, whether good or bad, triumphal or tragic, let my response reflect a God-honoring attitude of optimism, faith, and love for You. Amen

Day 10

ASK HIM

So I say to you, keep asking, and it will be given to you.
Keep searching, and you will find.
Keep knocking, and the door will be opened to you.
Luke 11:9 Holman CSB

God will help us become the people we are
meant to be, if only we will ask Him.
Hannah Whitall Smith

How often do you ask God for His help and His wisdom? Occasionally? Intermittently? Whenever you experience a crisis? Hopefully not. Hopefully, you've acquired the habit of asking for God's assistance early and often. And hopefully, you have learned to seek His guidance in every aspect of your life.

Jesus made it clear to His disciples: they should petition God to meet their needs. So should you. Genuine, heartfelt prayer produces powerful changes in you and in your world. When you lift your heart to God, you open yourself to a never-ending source of divine wisdom and infinite love.

James 5:16 makes a promise that God intends to keep: when you pray earnestly, fervently, and often, great things will happen. Too many people, however, are too timid or too pessimistic to ask God to do big things. Please don't count yourself among their number.

God can do great things through you if you have the courage to ask Him (and the determination to keep asking Him). But don't expect Him to do all the work. When you do your part, He will do His part—and when He does, you can expect miracles to happen.

The Bible promises that God will guide

you if you let Him. Your job is to let Him. But sometimes, you will be tempted to do otherwise. Sometimes, you'll be tempted to go along with the crowd; other times, you'll be tempted to do things your way, not God's way. When you feel those temptations, resist them.

God has promised that when you ask for His help, He will not withhold it. So ask. Ask Him to meet the needs of your day. Ask Him to lead you, to protect you, and to correct you. Then, trust the answers He gives.

God stands at the door and waits. When you knock, He opens. When you ask, He answers. Your task, of course, to make God a full partner in every aspect of your life—in good times and in hard times—and to seek His guidance prayerfully, confidently, and often.

TODAY'S TIP FOR HANDLING TOUGH TIMES

When you ask God for His assistance, He hears your request—and in His own time, He answers. If you need more, ask more.

More Powerful Ideas About Asking God

We sometimes fear to bring our troubles to God, because they must seem so small to him who sitteth on the circle of the earth. But, if they are large enough to vex and endanger our welfare, they are large enough to touch his heart of love.

R. A. Torrey

When will we realize that we're not troubling God with our questions and concerns? His heart is open to hear us—his touch nearer than our next thought—as if no one in the world existed but us. Our very personal God wants to hear from us personally.

Gigi Graham Tchividjian

All we have to do is to acknowledge our need, move from self-sufficiency to dependence, and ask God to become our hiding place.

Bill Hybels

Some people think God does not like to be troubled with our constant asking. But, the way to trouble God is not to come at all.

D. L. Moody

QUESTIONS TO CONSIDER

When I need more from life, do I ask more from God?

_____

_____

When I want to achieve a worthy goal, do I ask for God's help—and keep asking—until He answers my prayers?

_____

_____

Have I acquired the habit of asking for God's help many times each day?

_____

_____

A PRAYER FOR TODAY

Dear Lord, when I have questions or fears, I will turn to You. When I am weak, I will seek Your strength. When I am discouraged, Father, I will be mindful of Your love and Your grace. I will ask You for the things I need, Father, and I will trust Your answers, today and forever. Amen

Day 11

In Times of Uncertainty, Trust God's Timing

I waited patiently for the LORD;
And He inclined to me, and heard my cry.
Psalm 40:1 NKJV

Will not the Lord's time be
better than your time?
C. H. Spurgeon

The Bible teaches us to trust God's timing in all matters, but we are sorely tempted to do otherwise, especially when times are tough. When we are beset with problems, we are understandably anxious for a quick conclusion to our hardships. We know that our problems will end some day, and we want them to end NOW. God, however, works on His own timetable, and His schedule does not always coincide with ours.

God's plans are perfect; ours most certainly are not. So we must learn to trust the Father in good times and hard times. No exceptions.

Elisabeth Elliot advised, "We must learn to move according to the timetable of the Timeless One, and to be at peace." And Billy Graham observed, "As we wait on God, He helps us use the winds of adversity to soar above our problems."

So today, as you face the uncertainties of everyday life, do your best to turn everything over to God. Whatever "it" is, He can handle it. And you can be sure that He will handle it when the time is right.

PRAY FOR PATIENCE

Would you like to become a more patient person? Pray about it. Is there a person you dislike? Pray for a forgiving heart. Do you lose your temper more than you should? Ask God for help. Are you mired in the quicksand of regret? Ask God to liberate you.

As you pray more, you'll discover that God is always near and that He's always ready to hear from you. So don't worry about things; pray about them. God is waiting . . . and listening!

TODAY'S TIP FOR HANDLING TOUGH TIMES

God is in control of His world and your world. Rely upon Him. Vance Havner writes, "When we get to a place where it can't be done unless God does it, God will do it!" Enough said.

MORE POWERFUL IDEAS ABOUT GOD'S TIMING

By his wisdom, he orders his delays so that they prove to be far better than our hurries.

C. H. Spurgeon

God is in no hurry. Compared to the works of mankind, He is extremely deliberate. God is not a slave to the human clock.

Charles Swindoll

When we read of the great Biblical leaders, we see that it was not uncommon for God to ask them to wait, not just a day or two, but for years, until God was ready for them to act.

Gloria Gaither

We must leave it to God to answer our prayers in His own wisest way. Sometimes, we are so impatient and think that God does not answer. God always answers! He never fails! Be still. Abide in Him.

Mrs. Charles E. Cowman

QUESTIONS TO CONSIDER

Do I take seriously the Bible's instructions to be patient?

_____

_____

Do I believe that patience is not idle waiting but that it is an activity that means watching and waiting for God to lead me in the direction of His choosing?

_____

_____

Even when I don't understand the circumstances that confront me, do I strive to wait patiently while serving the Lord?

_____

_____

A PRAYER FOR TODAY

Dear Lord, Your timing is seldom my timing, but Your timing is always right for me. When I am impatient, remind me that You are never early or late. You are always on time, Lord . . . always. Amen

Day 12

MAKE PEACE WITH THE PAST

Peace I leave with you, my peace I give unto you:
not as the world giveth, give I unto you.
Let not your heart be troubled, neither let it be afraid.

John 14:27 KJV

If you are God's child, you are no longer bound
to your past or to what you were.
You are a brand new creature in Christ Jesus.

Kay Arthur

Some of life's greatest roadblocks are not the ones we see through the windshield; they are, instead, the roadblocks that seem to fill the rearview mirror. Because we are imperfect human beings who lack perfect control over our thoughts, we may allow ourselves to become "stuck" in the past—even though we know better. Instead of focusing our thoughts and energies on the opportunities of today, we may allow painful memories to fill our minds and sap our strength. We simply can't seem to let go of our pain, so we relive it again and again with predictably unfortunate consequences. Thankfully, God has other plans.

Philippians 3:13-14 instructs us to focus on the future, not the past: "One thing I do, forgetting those things which are behind and reaching forward to those things which are ahead, I press toward the goal for the prize of the upward call of God in Christ Jesus" (NKJV). Yet for many of us, focusing on the future is difficult indeed. Why? Part of the problem has to do with forgiveness. When we find ourselves focusing too intently on the past, it's a sure sign that we need to focus, instead, on a more urgent need: the need to forgive. Until we thoroughly and completely forgive those who have hurt us—and until we completely forgive. Focusing too intently on the past is, almost without exception, futile. No amount of anger or bitterness can change what happened yesterday. Tears can't change the past; regrets can't change it. Our worries won't change the past, and neither will our complaints. Simply put, the past is, and always will be, the past. Forever.

Once you have made peace with your past, you are free to become fully engaged in the present. And when you become fully engaged in the present, you are then free to build a better future for yourself and your loved ones.

If you've endured a difficult past, learn from it, but don't live in it. Instead, build your future on a firm foundation of trust and forgiveness: trust in your Heavenly Father, and forgiveness for all His children, including yourself. Give all your yesterdays to God, and celebrate this day with hope in your heart and praise on your lips. Your Creator intends to use you in wonderful, unexpected ways if you let Him. But first, God wants you to make peace with your past . . . and He wants you to do it now.

TODAY'S TIP FOR HANDLING TOUGH TIMES

The past is past, so don't invest all your energy there. If you're focused on the past, change your focus. If you're living in the past, it's time to stop living there.

MORE FROM GOD'S WORD ABOUT THE PAST

Do not remember the past events, pay no attention to things of old. Look, I am about to do something new; even now it is coming. Do you not see it? Indeed, I will make a way in the wilderness, rivers in the desert.

Isaiah 43:18-19 Holman CSB

Brothers, I do not consider myself to have taken hold of it. But one thing I do: forgetting what is behind and reaching forward to what is ahead, I pursue as my goal the prize promised by God's heavenly call in Christ Jesus.

Philippians 3:13-14 Holman CSB

QUESTIONS TO CONSIDER

Am I able to learn from the past and to accept the past, but to live in the present?

_____

_____

Do I believe that it is important to trust God even when I don't understand why certain things happen?

_____

_____

Am I willing to change the things I can change and accept the things I can't?

_____

_____

A PRAYER FOR TODAY

Heavenly Father, free me from anger, resentment, and envy. When I am bitter, I cannot feel the peace that You intend for my life. Keep me mindful that forgiveness is Your commandment, and help me accept the past, treasure the present, and trust the future to You. Amen

Day 13

IN TIMES OF UNCERTAINTY, KEEP PRAYING

Is anyone among you suffering? He should pray.
Is anyone cheerful? He should sing praises.
James 5:13 Holman CSB

I have found the perfect antidote for fear.
Whenever it sticks up its ugly face,
I clobber it with prayer.
Dale Evans Rogers

God is trying to get His message through to you! Are you listening?

Perhaps, if you're experiencing tough times or uncertain times, you may find yourself overwhelmed by the press of everyday life. Perhaps you forget to slow yourself down long enough to talk with God. Instead of turning your thoughts and prayers to Him, you may rely upon our own resources. Instead of asking God for guidance, you may depend only upon your own limited wisdom. A far better course of action is this: simply stop what you're doing long enough to open your heart to God; then listen carefully for His directions.

Do you spend time each day with God? You should. Are you in need? Ask God to sustain you. Are you troubled? Take your worries to Him in prayer. Are you weary? Seek God's strength. In all things great and small, seek God's wisdom and His grace. He hears your prayers, and He will answer. All you must do is ask.

GOT QUESTIONS?

You've got questions? God's got answers. And if you'd like to hear from Him, here's precisely what you must do: petition Him with a sincere heart; be still; be patient; and listen. Then, in His own time and in His own fashion, God will answer your questions and give you guidance for the journey ahead.

Today, turn over everything to your Creator. Pray constantly about matters great and small. Seek God's instruction and His direction. And remember: God always hears your prayers and answers them.

TODAY'S TIP FOR HANDLING TOUGH TIMES

Sometimes, the answer is "No." God does not answer all of our prayers in the affirmative, nor should He. His job is not to grant all our earthly requests; His job is to offer us eternal salvation (for which we must be eternally grateful). When we are disappointed by the realities of life-here-on-earth, we should remember that our prayers are always answered by a sovereign, all-knowing God, and that we must trust Him, whether He answers "Yes," "No," or "Not yet."

MORE POWERFUL IDEAS ABOUT PRAYER

God always answers the prayers of His children—
but His answer isn't always "Yes."

Billy Graham

I have witnessed many attitudes make a positive
turnaround through prayer.

John Maxwell

Real power in prayer flows only when a man's
spirit touches God's spirit.

Catherine Marshall

Any concern that is too small to be turned into a
prayer is too small to be made into a burden.

Corrie ten Boom

When we pray, we have linked ourselves with
Divine purposes, and we therefore have Divine
power at our disposal for human living.

E. Stanley Jones

Prayer accomplishes more than anything else.

Bill Bright

QUESTIONS TO CONSIDER

Do I understand that prayer strengthens my relationship with God?

_____

_____

Do I trust that God will care for me, even when it seems that my prayers have gone unanswered?

_____

_____

Do I believe that my prayers have the power to change my circumstances, my perspective, and my future?

_____

_____

A PRAYER FOR TODAY

Dear Lord, let me raise my hopes and my dreams, my worries and my fears to You. Let me be a worthy example to family and friends, showing them the importance and the power of prayer. Let me take everything to You in prayer, Lord, and when I do, let me trust in Your answers. Amen

Day 14

GOD'S PROTECTION

Though I sit in darkness, the Lord will be my light.
Micah 7:8 Holman CSB

God helps those who help themselves,
but there are times when we are quite incapable
of helping ourselves. That's when God
stoops down and gathers us in His arms like
a mother lifts a sick child, and does for us
what we cannot do for ourselves.
Ruth Bell Graham

Have you ever faced challenges that seemed too big to handle? Have you ever faced big problems that, despite your best efforts, simply could not be solved? If so, you know how uncomfortable it is to feel helpless in the face of difficult circumstances. Thankfully, even when there's nowhere else to turn, you can turn your thoughts and prayers to God, and He will respond.

God's hand uplifts those who turn their hearts and prayers to Him. Count yourself among that number. When you do, you can live courageously and joyfully, knowing that "this too will pass"— but that God's love for you will not. And you can draw strength from the knowledge that you are a marvelous creation, loved, protected, and uplifted by the ever-present hand of God.

OPEN YOUR HEART TO HIM

St. Augustine observed, "God loves each of us as if there were only one of us." Do you believe those words? Do you seek to have an intimate, one-on-one relationship with your Heavenly Father, or are you satisfied to keep Him at a "safe" distance?

Sometimes, in the crush of our daily duties, God may seem far away, but He is not. God is everywhere we have ever been and everywhere we will ever go. He is with us night and day; He knows our thoughts and our prayers. And, when we earnestly seek Him, we will find Him because He is here, waiting patiently for us to reach out to Him.

Today, as you carve out quiet moments of thanksgiving and praise for your Heavenly Father, open yourself to His presence and to His love. He is here, waiting. His love is here, always. Accept it—now—and be blessed.

TODAY'S TIP FOR HANDLING TOUGH TIMES

In dealing with difficult situations, view God as your comfort and your strength. Through good times and bad, God is always with you, and you are always protected.

QUESTIONS TO CONSIDER

Do I believe that God will protect me now and throughout eternity?

_____

_____

Do I trust God's plans even when I cannot understand them?

_____

_____

Am I willing to accept God's unfolding plan for the world—and for my world?

_____

_____

A PRAYER FOR TODAY

Lord, sometimes life is difficult. Sometimes, I am worried, weary, or heartbroken. And sometimes, I encounter powerful temptations to disobey Your commandments. But, when I lift my eyes to You, Father, You strengthen me. When I am weak, You lift me up. Today, I will turn to You for strength, for hope, for direction, and for deliverance. Amen

Day 15

ACCEPTING
ADVICE

A wise man will hear and increase learning,
and a man of understanding will attain wise counsel.
Proverbs 1:5 NKJV

It takes a wise person to give good advice,
but an even wiser person to take it.
Marie T. Freeman

If you find yourself caught up in a difficult situation, it's time to start searching for knowledgeable friends and mentors who can give you solid advice. Why do you need help evaluating the person in the mirror? Because you're simply too close to that person, that's why. Sometimes, you'll be tempted to give yourself straight A's when you deserve considerably lower grades. On other occasions, you'll become your own worst critic, giving yourself a string of failing marks when you deserve better. The truth, of course, is often somewhere in the middle.

Finding a wise mentor is only half the battle. It takes just as much wisdom—and sometimes more—to act upon good advice as it does to give it. So find people you can trust, listen to them carefully, and act accordingly.

FIND A MENTOR

If you're going through tough times or uncertain times, it's helpful to find mentors who have been there, and done that—people who have experienced your particular challenge and lived to tell about it.

When you find mentors who are godly men and women, you become a more godly person yourself. That's why you should seek out advisers who, by their words and their presence, make you a better person and a better Christian.

Today, as a gift to yourself, select, from your friends and family members, a mentor whose judgment you trust. Then listen carefully to your mentor's advice and be willing to accept that advice, even if accepting it requires effort or pain, or both. Consider your mentor to be God's gift to you. Thank God for that gift, and use it for the glory of His kingdom.

TODAY'S TIP FOR HANDLING TOUGH TIMES

If you can't seem to listen to constructive criticism with an open mind, perhaps you've got a severe case of old-fashioned stubbornness. If so, ask God to soften your heart, open your ears, and enlighten your mind.

MORE FROM GOD'S WORD ABOUT
ACCEPTING ADVICE

Listen to counsel and receive instruction so that you may be wise in later life.

Proverbs 19:20 Holman CSB

It is better to listen to rebuke from a wise person than to listen to the song of fools.

Ecclesiastes 7:5 Holman CSB

An ear that listens to life-giving rebukes will be at home among the wise.

Proverbs 15:31 Holman CSB

The one who walks with the wise will become wise, but a companion of fools will suffer harm.

Proverbs 13:20 Holman CSB

The way of a fool is right in his own eyes, but he who heeds counsel is wise.

Proverbs 12:15 NKJV

QUESTIONS TO CONSIDER

Do I understand the importance of finding—and listening to—mentors?

_____

_____

Am I willing to be a mentor to others?

_____

_____

Am I willing to listen carefully to advice and, when appropriate, to take it? Or am I a little too stubborn to take advice from others?

_____

_____

A PRAYER FOR TODAY

Dear Lord, thank You for the mentors whom You have placed along my path. When I am troubled, let me turn to them for help, for guidance, for comfort, and for perspective. And Father, let me be a friend and mentor to others, so that my love for You may be demonstrated by my genuine concern for them. Amen

Day 16

SELF-ESTEEM
ACCORDING
TO GOD

For you made us only a little lower than God,
and you crowned us with glory and honor.
Psalm 8:5 NLT

Being loved by Him whose opinion matters most
gives us the security to risk loving, too—
even loving ourselves.
Gloria Gaither

When you encounter tough times, you may lose self-confidence. Or you may become so focused on what other people are thinking—or saying—that you fail to focus on God. To do so is a mistake of major proportions—don't make it. Instead, seek God's guidance as you focus your energies on becoming the best you that you can possibly be. And when it comes to matters of self-esteem and self-image, seek approval not from your peers, but from your Creator.

Millions of words have been written about various ways to improve self-image and increase self-esteem. Yet, maintaining a healthy self-image is, to a surprising extent, a matter of doing three things: 1. Obeying God 2. Thinking healthy thoughts 3. Finding a purpose for your life that pleases your Creator and yourself. The following common-sense, Biblically-based tips can help you build the kind of self-image—and the kind of life—that both you and God can be proud of:

1. Do the right thing: If you're misbehaving, how can you possibly hope to feel good about yourself? (See Romans 14:12)

2. Watch what you think: If your inner voice is, in reality, your inner critic, you need to tone down

the criticism now. And while you're at it, train yourself to begin thinking thoughts that are more rational, more accepting, and less judgmental. (Philippians 4:8)

3. Spend time with boosters, not critics: Are your friends putting you down? If so, find new friends. (Hebrews 3:13)

4. Don't be a perfectionist: Strive for excellence, but never confuse it with perfection. (Ecclesiastes 11:4,6)

5. If you're addicted to something unhealthy, stop; if you can't stop, get help: Addictions, of whatever type, create havoc in your life. And disorder. And grief. And low self-esteem. (Exodus 20:3)

6. Find a purpose for your life that is larger than you are: When you're dedicated to something or someone besides yourself, you blossom. (Ephesians 6:7)

7. Don't worry too much about self-esteem: Instead, worry more about living a life that is pleasing to God. Learn to think optimistically. Find a worthy purpose. Find people to love and people to serve. When you do, your self-esteem will, on most days, take care of itself.

More Powerful Ideas About Your Self-Worth

As you and I lay up for ourselves living, lasting treasures in Heaven, we come to the awesome conclusion that we ourselves are His treasure!

Anne Graham Lotz

When it comes to our position before God, we're perfect. When he sees each of us, he sees one who has been made perfect through the One who is perfect—Jesus Christ.

Max Lucado

Give yourself a gift today: be present with yourself. God is. Enjoy your own personality. God does.

Barbara Johnson

Today's Tip for Handling Tough Times

Don't make the mistake of selling yourself short. No matter the size of your challenges, you can be sure that you and God, working together, can tackle them.

QUESTIONS TO CONSIDER

Do I pay careful attention to the messages that I'm sending myself about myself?

_____

_____

Am I sometimes my own worst critic, and is the criticism really deserved?

_____

_____

Do I remind myself that God loves me . . . and that I should, too?

_____

_____

A PRAYER FOR TODAY

Dear Lord, help me speak courteously to everyone, including myself. And when I make a mistake, help me to forgive myself quickly and thoroughly, just as I forgive others. Amen

Day 17

In Times of Uncertainty, Guard Your Thoughts

Finally brothers, whatever is true, whatever is honorable, whatever is just, whatever is pure, whatever is lovely, whatever is commendable— if there is any moral excellence and if there is any praise—dwell on these things.

Philippians 4:8 Holman CSB

Your thoughts are the determining factor as to whose mold you are conformed to. Control your thoughts and you control the direction of your life.

Charles Stanley

Are you an optimistic, hopeful, enthusiastic Christian? You should be. After all, as a believer, you have every reason to be optimistic about life here on earth and life eternal. As English clergyman William Ralph Inge observed, "No Christian should be a pessimist, for Christianity is a system of radical optimism." Inge's words are most certainly true, but sometimes, you may find yourself pulled down by tough times. If you find yourself discouraged, exhausted, or both, then it's time to ask yourself this question: what's bothering you, and why?

If you're worried by the inevitable challenges of everyday living, God wants to have a little talk with you. After all, the ultimate battle has already been won on the cross at Calvary. And if your life has been transformed by Christ's sacrifice, then you, as a recipient of God's grace, have every reason to live courageously.

A. W. Tozer noted, "Attitude is all-important. Let the soul take a quiet attitude of faith and love toward God, and from there on, the responsibility is God's. He will make good on His commitments." These words should serve as a reminder that even when the challenges of the day seem daunting, God remains steadfast. And, so should you.

So make this promise to yourself and keep it—vow to be a hope-filled Christian. Think optimistically about your life, your profession, your family, your future, and your purpose for living. Trust your hopes, not your fears. Take time to celebrate God's glorious creation. And then, when you've filled your heart with hope and gladness, share your optimism with others. They'll be better for it, and so will you.

TODAY'S TIP FOR HANDLING TOUGH TIMES

Be a realistic optimist. Your attitude toward the future will help create your future. So think realistically about yourself and your situation while making a conscious effort to focus on hopes, not fears. When you do, you'll put the self-fulfilling prophecy to work for you.

QUESTIONS TO CONSIDER

Do I understand the importance of directing my thoughts in a proper direction?

_____

_____

Do I believe that emotions are contagious, and do I try to associate with people who are upbeat, optimistic, and encouraging?

_____

_____

Do I understand that when I dwell on positive thoughts, I feel better about myself and my circumstances?

_____

_____

A PRAYER FOR TODAY

Dear Lord, I will focus on Your love, Your power, Your promises, and Your Son. When I am weak, I will turn to You for strength; when I am troubled, I will turn to You for patience and perspective. Help me guard my thoughts, Lord, so that I may honor You this day and forever. Amen

Day 18

IN TIMES OF UNCERTAINTY, STUDY GOD'S WORD

All Scripture is inspired by God and is profitable for teaching, for rebuking, for correcting, for training in righteousness, so that the man of God may be complete, equipped for every good work.

2 Timothy 3:16-17 Holman CSB

The strength that we claim from God's Word does not depend on circumstances. Circumstances will be difficult, but our strength will be sufficient.

Corrie ten Boom

The words of Matthew 4:4 remind us that, "Man shall not live by bread alone but by every word that proceedeth out of the mouth of God." (KJV). As believers, we must study the Bible and meditate upon its meaning for our lives. Otherwise, we deprive ourselves of a priceless gift from our Creator.

God's Word is unlike any other book. The Bible is a roadmap for life here on earth and for life eternal. As Christians, we are called upon to study God's Holy Word, to follow its commandments, and to share its Good News with the world.

Jonathan Edwards advised, "Be assiduous in reading the Holy Scriptures. This is the fountain whence all knowledge in divinity must be derived. Therefore let not this treasure lie by you neglected." God's Holy Word is, indeed, a priceless, one-of-a-kind treasure, and a passing acquaintance with the Good Book is insufficient for Christians who seek to obey God's Word and to understand His will. After all, man does not live by bread alone . . .

GOD'S WORD REDUCES STRESS

If you're experiencing stress, God's Word can help relieve it. And if you'd like to experience God's peace, Bible study can help provide it.

Warren Wiersbe observed, "When the child of God looks into the Word of God, he sees the Son of God. And, he is transformed by the Spirit of God to share in the glory of God." God's Holy Word is, indeed, life-changing, stress-reducing, and a one-of-a-kind treasure. And it's up to you—and only you—to use it that way.

TODAY'S TIP FOR HANDLING TOUGH TIMES

If you have a choice to make, the Bible can help you make it. If you've got questions, the Bible has answers. So take a Bible with you wherever you go. You never know when you may need a midday spiritual pick-me-up.

MORE POWERFUL IDEAS ABOUT GOD'S WORD

God has given us all sorts of counsel and direction in his written Word; thank God, we have it written down in black and white.

John Eldredge

Weave the fabric of God's word through your heart and mind. It will hold strong, even if the rest of life unravels.

Gigi Graham Tchividjian

The Bible is God's Word, given to us by God Himself so we can know Him and His will for our lives.

Billy Graham

Nobody ever outgrows Scripture; the book widens and deepens with our years.

C. H. Spurgeon

Prayer and the Word are inseparably linked together. Power in the use of either depends on the presence of the other.

Andrew Murray

QUESTIONS TO CONSIDER

Do I make it a priority to read the Bible every day?

_____

_____

Do I consider regular Bible study to be an important source of wisdom?

_____

_____

Do I have a systematic plan for studying of God's Word?

_____

_____

A PRAYER FOR TODAY

Heavenly Father, Your Word is a light unto the world; I will study it and trust it, and share it. In all that I do, help me be a worthy witness for You as I share the Good News of Your perfect Son and Your perfect Word. Amen

Day 19

In Times of Uncertainty, Don't Give Up!

*For a righteous man may
fall seven times and rise again.*

Proverbs 24:16 NKJV

We don't give up. We look up. We trust.
We believe. And our optimism is not hollow.
Christ has proven worthy. He has shown that
he never fails. That's what makes God, God.

Max Lucado

The old saying is as true today as it was when it was first spoken: "Life is a marathon, not a sprint." That's why wise travelers (like you) select a traveling companion who never tires and never falters. That partner, of course, is your Heavenly Father.

The next time you find your courage tested to the limit, remember that God is as near as your next breath, and remember that He offers strength and comfort to His children. He is your shield and your strength; He is your protector and your deliverer. Call upon Him in your hour of need and then be comforted. Whatever your challenge, whatever your trouble, God can help you persevere. And that's precisely what He'll do if you ask Him.

Perhaps you are in a hurry for God to help you resolve your difficulties. Perhaps you're anxious to earn the rewards that you feel you've already earned from life. Perhaps you're drumming your fingers, impatiently waiting for God to act. If so, be forewarned: God operates on His own timetable, not yours. Sometimes, God may answer your prayers with silence, and when He does, you must patiently persevere. In times of trouble, you must remain steadfast and trust in the merciful goodness of your Heavenly Father. Whatever your problem, He can handle it. Your job is to keep persevering until He does.

TODAY'S TIP FOR HANDLING TOUGH TIMES

Are you being tested? Call upon God. The next time you find your courage tested to the limit, remember that God is as near as your next breath, and remember that He offers strength and comfort to His children. He is your shield, your protector, and your deliverer. Call upon Him in your hour of need and then be comforted. Whatever your challenge, whatever your trouble, God can give you the strength to persevere, and that's exactly what you should ask Him to do.

MORE POWERFUL IDEAS ABOUT PERSEVERANCE

Failure is one of life's most powerful teachers. How we handle our failures determines whether we're going to simply "get by" in life or "press on."

Beth Moore

As we wait on God, He helps us use the winds of adversity to soar above our problems. As the Bible says, "Those who wait on the LORD . . . shall mount up with wings like eagles."

Billy Graham

In all negotiations of difficulties, a man may not look to sow and reap at once. He must prepare his business and so ripen it by degrees.

Francis Bacon

Are you a Christian? If you are, how can you be hopeless? Are you so depressed by the greatness of your problems that you have given up all hope? Instead of giving up, would you patiently endure? Would you focus on Christ until you are so preoccupied with him alone that you fall prostrate before him?

Anne Graham Lotz

QUESTIONS TO CONSIDER

Do I have a healthy respect for the power of perseverance?

_____

_____

When I am discouraged, do I ask God to give me strength?

_____

_____

Do I associate with people who encourage me to be courageous, optimistic, energetic, and persistent?

_____

_____

A PRAYER FOR TODAY

Lord, when life is difficult, I am tempted to abandon hope in the future. But You are my God, and I can draw strength from You. Let me trust You, Father, in good times and in bad times. Let me persevere—even if my soul is troubled—and let me follow Your Son, Jesus Christ, this day and forever. Amen

Day 20

LIVE
COURAGEOUSLY

He will not fear bad news; his heart is confident,
trusting in the Lord. His heart is assured;
he will not fear.

Psalm 112:7-8 Holman CSB

Faith not only can help you through a crisis,
it can help you to approach life after
the hard times with a whole new perspective.
It can help you adopt an outlook of hope and
courage through faith to face reality.

John Maxwell

Every person's life is a tapestry of events: some wonderful, some not-so-wonderful, and some downright disastrous. When we visit the mountaintops of life, praising God isn't hard—in fact, it's easy. In our moments of triumph, we can bow our heads and thank God for our victories. But when we fail to reach the mountaintops, when we endure the inevitable losses that are a part of every person's life, we find it much tougher to give God the praise He deserves. Yet wherever we find ourselves, whether on the mountaintops of life or in life's darkest valleys, we must still offer thanks to God, giving thanks in all circumstances.

The next time you find yourself worried about the challenges of today or the uncertainties of tomorrow, ask yourself this question: are you really ready to place your concerns and your life in God's all-powerful, all-knowing, all-loving hands? If the answer to that question is yes—as it should be—then you can draw courage today from the source of strength that never fails: your Father in heaven.

God is with you always, listening to your thoughts and prayers, watching over your every move. If the demands of everyday life weigh down upon you, you may be tempted to ignore God's presence or—worse yet—to lose faith in His promises. But, when you quiet yourself and acknowledge His presence, God will touch your heart and restore your courage.

At this very moment—as you're fulfilling your obligations and overcoming tough times—God is seeking to work in you and through you. He's asking you to live abundantly and courageously and He's ready to help. So why not let Him do it . . . starting now?

TODAY'S TIP FOR HANDLING TOUGH TIMES

With God as your partner, you have nothing to fear. Why? Because you and God, working together, can handle absolutely anything that comes your way. So the next time you'd like an extra measure of courage, recommit yourself to a true one-on-one relationship with your Creator. When you sincerely turn to Him, He will never fail you.

More from God's Word About Courage

Be strong and courageous, and do the work. Don't be afraid or discouraged, for the Lord God, my God, is with you. He won't leave you or forsake you.

1 Chronicles 28:20 Holman CSB

For God has not given us a spirit of fearfulness, but one of power, love, and sound judgment.

2 Timothy 1:7 Holman CSB

Be alert, stand firm in the faith, be brave and strong.

1 Corinthians 16:13 Holman CSB

Haven't I commanded you: be strong and courageous? Do not be afraid or discouraged, for the Lord your God is with you wherever you go.

Joshua 1:9 Holman CSB

But when Jesus heard it, He answered him, "Don't be afraid. Only believe."

Luke 8:50 Holman CSB

QUESTIONS TO CONSIDER

Do I consider God to be my partner in every aspect of my life?

_____

_____

Do I trust God to handle the problems that are simply too big for me to solve?

_____

_____

Am I really willing to place the future—and my future—in God's hands?

_____

_____

A PRAYER FOR TODAY

Lord, sometimes I face challenges that leave me breathless. When I am fearful, let me lean upon You. With You by my side, I have nothing to fear. And, with Your Son Jesus as my Savior, I have received the priceless gift of eternal life. Help me to be a grateful and courageous servant this day and every day. Amen

Day 21

YOU'RE NEVER ALONE

The Lord is the One who will go before you.
He will be with you;
He will not leave you or forsake you.
Do not be afraid or discouraged.

Deuteronomy 31:8 Holman CSB

God is in the midst of whatever has happened,
is happening, and will happen.

Charles Swindoll

If God is everywhere, why does He sometimes seem to be so far away? The answer to that question, of course, has nothing to do with God and everything to do with us.

When we begin each day on our knees, in praise and worship to Him, God often seems very near indeed. But, if we ignore God's presence or—worse yet—rebel against it altogether, the world in which we live becomes a spiritual wasteland.

Are you tired, discouraged, or fearful? Be comforted because God is with you. Are you confused? Listen to the quiet voice of your Heavenly Father. Are you bitter? Talk with God and seek His guidance. Are you celebrating a great victory? Thank God and praise Him. He is the Giver of all things good.

In whatever condition you find yourself, wherever you are, whether you are happy or sad, victorious or vanquished, troubled or triumphant, celebrate God's presence. And be comforted. God is not just near. He is here.

SPENDING QUIET MOMENTS WITH GOD

We live in uncertain times, and the demands of everyday life can seem overwhelming. But when we slow ourselves down and seek the presence of a loving God, we invite His peace into our hearts.

Do you set aside quiet moments each day to offer praise to your Creator? You should. During these moments of stillness, you will often sense the infinite love and power of our Lord.

The familiar words of Psalm 46:10 remind us to "Be still, and know that I am God." When we do so, we encounter the awesome presence of our loving Heavenly Father, and we are comforted in the knowledge that God is not just near. He is here.

TODAY'S TIP FOR HANDLING TOUGH TIMES

Having trouble hearing God? If so, slow yourself down, tune out the distractions, and listen carefully. God has important things to say; your task is to be still and listen.

MORE POWERFUL IDEAS ABOUT GOD'S PRESENCE

God's silence is in no way indicative of His activity or involvement in our lives. He may be silent, but He is not still.

Charles Swindoll

We should learn to live in the presence of the living God. He should be a well for us: delightful, comforting, unfailing, springing up to eternal life (John 4:14). When we rely on other people, their water supplies ultimately dry up. But, the well of the Creator never fails to nourish us.

C. H. Spurgeon

Certainly, God is with us in times of distress, and that is a comforting truth. But listen: Jesus wants to be part of every experience and every moment of our lives.

Billy Graham

Get yourself into the presence of the loving Father. Just place yourself before Him, and look up into, His face; think of His love, His wonderful, tender, pitying love.

Andrew Murray

QUESTIONS TO CONSIDER

Do I believe that God seeks a close and intimate relationship with me?

_____

_____

Do I understand that whenever I feel distance from God, that distance is my own doing, not His?

_____

_____

Am I willing to quiet myself long enough to sense God's presence and His love?

_____

_____

A PRAYER FOR TODAY

Heavenly Father, even when it seems to me that You are far away, You never leave my side. Today and every day, I will strive to feel Your presence, and I will strive to sense Your love for me. Amen

Day 22

WORSHIP HIM EVERY DAY

God is Spirit, and those who worship Him must worship in spirit and truth.
John 4:24 Holman CSB

When your grief presses you to the very dust, worship there.
C. H. Spurgeon

Do you take time each day to worship your Father in heaven, or do you wait until Sunday morning to praise Him for His blessings? The answer to this question will, in large part, determine the quality and direction of your spiritual life.

When we worship God every day of our lives, we are blessed. When we fail to worship God, for whatever reason, we forfeit the spiritual gifts that He intends for us.

Every day provides opportunities to put God where He belongs: at the center of our lives. When we do so, we worship Him not only with our words, but also with our deeds, and that's as it should be. For believers, God comes first. Always first.

ALWAYS GIVE THANKS

The words of 1 Thessalonians 5:18 remind us to give thanks in every circumstance of life. But sometimes, when our hearts are troubled and our lives seem to be spinning out of control, we don't feel much like thanking the Creator (or anybody else for that matter). Yet God's Word is clear: In all circumstances, our Father offers us His love, His strength, and His grace. And, in all circumstances, we must thank Him.

Have you thanked God today for blessings that are too numerous to count? Have you offered Him your heartfelt prayers and your wholehearted praise? If not, it's time to slow down and offer a prayer of thanksgiving to the One who has given you life on earth and life eternal.

If you are a thoughtful Christian, you will be a thankful Christian. No matter your circumstances, you owe God so much more than you can ever repay, and you owe Him your heartfelt thanks. So thank Him . . . and keep thanking Him, today, tomorrow and forever.

TODAY'S TIP FOR HANDLING TOUGH TIMES

Worship reminds you of an important truth: God is big enough to handle your problems. But that's not all: When you worship God with a sincere heart, He will guide your steps and bless your life.

MORE FROM GOD'S WORD ABOUT WORSHIP

But an hour is coming, and is now here, when the true worshipers will worship the Father in spirit and truth. Yes, the Father wants such people to worship Him. God is Spirit, and those who worship Him must worship in spirit and truth."

John 4:23-24 Holman CSB

So that at the name of Jesus every knee should bow— of those who are in heaven and on earth and under the earth—and every tongue should confess that Jesus Christ is Lord, to the glory of God the Father.

Philippians 2:10-11 Holman CSB

Worship the Lord your God and . . . serve Him only.

Matthew 4:10 Holman CSB

If anyone is thirsty, he should come to Me and drink!

John 7:37 Holman CSB

I rejoiced with those who said to me, "Let us go to the house of the Lord."

Psalm 122:1 Holman CSB

QUESTIONS TO CONSIDER

Do I believe that it is important to worship God every day of the week, not just on Sundays?

_____

_____

Do I feel that it is important to worship regularly with the community of believers?

_____

_____

Do I have a quiet place where I can go, a place where God seems especially close?

_____

_____

A PRAYER FOR TODAY

Heavenly Father, let today and every day be a time of worship. Let me worship You, not only with words and deeds, but also with my heart. In the quiet moments of the day, let me praise You and thank You for creating me, loving me, guiding me, and saving me. Amen

Day 23

THE NEED TO FORGIVE

All bitterness, anger and wrath, insult and slander
must be removed from you, along with
all wickedness. And be kind and compassionate
to one another, forgiving one another,
just as God also forgave you in Christ.

Ephesians 4:31-32 Holman CSB

To be a Christian means
to forgive the inexcusable, because
God has forgiven the inexcusable in you.

C. S. Lewis

It has been said that life is an exercise in forgiveness. And it should be added that forgiveness is an essential step in overcoming tough times.

Christ understood the importance of forgiveness when he commanded, "Love your enemies and pray for those who persecute you" (Matthew 5:43-44 NIV). But sometimes, forgiveness is difficult indeed.

When we have been injured or embarrassed, we feel the urge to strike back and to hurt the ones who have hurt us. But Christ instructs us to do otherwise. Christ teaches us that forgiveness is God's way and that mercy is an integral part of God's plan for our lives. In short, we are commanded to weave the thread of forgiveness into the very fabric of our lives.

Do you invest more time than you should reliving the past? Are you troubled by feelings of anger, bitterness, envy, or regret? Do you harbor ill will against someone whom you simply can't seem to forgive? If so, it's time to finally get serious about forgiveness.

When someone hurts you, the act of forgiveness is difficult, but necessary. Until you forgive, you are trapped in a prison of your own creation.

But what if you have tried to forgive and simply can't seem to do so? The solution to your dilemma is this: you simply must make forgiveness a higher priority in your life.

Most of us don't spend too much time thinking about forgiveness; we worry, instead, about the injustices we have suffered and the people who inflicted them. God has a better plan: He wants us to live in the present, not the past, and He knows that in order to do so, we must forgive those who have harmed us.

Have you made forgiveness a high priority? Have you sincerely asked God to forgive you for your inability to forgive others? Have you genuinely prayed that those feelings of anger might be swept from your heart? Is so, congratulations. If not, perhaps it's time to move past your own particular tough times by freeing yourself from the chains of bitterness and regret.

A person's insight gives him patience,
and his virtue is to overlook an offense.

—

Proverbs 19:11 Holman CSB

MORE POWERFUL IDEAS ABOUT
THE NEED TO FORGIVE

God expects us to forgive others as He has forgiven us; we are to follow His example by having a forgiving heart.

Vonette Bright

Forgiveness is actually the best revenge because it not only sets us free from the person we forgive, but it frees us to move into all that God has in store for us.

Stormie Omartian

TODAY'S TIP FOR HANDLING TOUGH TIMES

Today, think about the people you still need to forgive. And then ask God to help you forgive them. Remember that when you forgive other people, you're giving yourself a gift. And, remember that God doesn't say that forgiveness is optional; it's a commandment.

QUESTIONS TO CONSIDER

Am I willing to acknowledge the important role that forgiveness should play in my life?

_____

_____

Will I strive to forgive those who have hurt me, even when doing so is difficult?

_____

_____

Do I understand that forgiveness is a marathon (not a sprint), and will I prayerfully ask God to help me move beyond the emotions of bitterness and regret?

_____

_____

A PRAYER FOR TODAY

Heavenly Father, forgiveness is Your commandment, and I know that I should forgive others just as You have forgiven me. But, genuine forgiveness is difficult. Help me to forgive those who have injured me, and deliver me from the traps of anger and bitterness. Forgiveness is Your way, Lord; let it be mine. Amen

Day 24

FINDING STRENGTH IN TIMES OF UNCERTAINTY

I can do all things through Christ who strengthens me.
Philippians 4:13 NKJV

When trials come your way—as inevitably they will—
do not run away. Run to your God and Father.
Kay Arthur

God's love and support never changes. From the cradle to the grave, God has promised to give you the strength to meet any challenge. God has promised to lift you up and guide your steps if you let Him. God has promised that when you entrust your life to Him completely and without reservation, He will give you the courage to face any trial and the wisdom to live in His righteousness.

God's hand uplifts those who turn their hearts and prayers to Him. Will you count yourself among that number? Will you accept God's peace and wear God's armor against the temptations and distractions of our dangerous world? If you do, you can live courageously and optimistically, knowing that you have been forever touched by the loving, unfailing, uplifting hand of God.

HE IS SUFFICIENT

Of this you can be certain: God is sufficient to meet your needs. Period.

Do the demands of life seem overwhelming at times? If so, you must learn to rely not only upon your own resources, but also upon the promises of your Father in heaven. God will hold your hand and walk with you and your family if you let Him. So even if your circumstances are difficult, trust the Father.

God promises that He is "near to those who have a broken heart" (Psalm 34:18 NKJV). When we are troubled, we must turn to Him, and we must encourage our friends and family members to do likewise.

If you are discouraged by the inevitable demands of life here on earth, be mindful of this fact: the loving heart of God is sufficient to meet any challenge . . . including yours.

TODAY'S TIP FOR HANDLING TOUGH TIMES

The next time you're tempted to give up on yourself, remember that God will never, never, never give up on you. And with God in your corner, you have nothing to fear.

MORE POWERFUL IDEAS ABOUT
FINDING STRENGTH

The same God who empowered Samson, Gideon, and Paul seeks to empower my life and your life, because God hasn't changed.

Bill Hybels

A divine strength is given to those who yield themselves to the Father and obey what He tells them to do.

Warren Wiersbe

No matter how heavy the burden, daily strength is given, so I expect we need not give ourselves any concern as to what the outcome will be. We must simply go forward.

Annie Armstrong

All the power of God—the same power that hung the stars in place and put the planets in their courses and transformed Earth—now resides in you to energize and strengthen you to become the person God created you to be.

Anne Graham Lotz

QUESTIONS TO CONSIDER

Do I gain strength and courage when I allow Christ to dwell in the center of my heart?

_____

_____

Do I gain strength through prayer?

_____

_____

Do I understand the importance of regular exercise and sensible rest?

_____

_____

A PRAYER FOR TODAY

Lord, sometimes life is difficult. Sometimes, I am worried, weary, or heartbroken. But, when I lift my eyes to You, Father, You strengthen me. When I am weak, You lift me up. Today, I turn to You, Lord, for my strength, for my hope, and my salvation. Amen

Day 25

IN TIMES OF UNCERTAINTY, WE MAY BE TOO FOCUSED ON POSSESSIONS

Don't collect for yourselves treasures on earth, where moth and rust destroy and where thieves break in and steal. But collect for yourselves treasures in heaven, where neither moth nor rust destroys, and where thieves don't break in and steal. For where your treasure is, there your heart will be also.

Matthew 6:19-21 Holman CSB

True contentment comes from godliness in the heart, not from wealth in the hand.

Warren Wiersbe

All too often we focus our thoughts and energies on the accumulation of earthly treasures, creating untold stress in our lives and leaving precious little time to accumulate the only treasures that really matter: the spiritual kind. Our material possessions have the potential to do great good—depending upon how we use them. If we allow the things we own to own us, we may pay dearly for our misplaced priorities.

Society focuses intently on material possessions, but God's Word teaches us time and again that money matters little when compared to the spiritual gifts that the Creator offers to those who put Him first in their lives. So today, keep your possessions in perspective. Remember that God should come first, and everything else next. When you give God His rightful place in your heart, you'll have a clearer vision of the things that really matter. Then, you can joyfully thank your Heavenly Father for spiritual blessings that are, in truth, too numerous to count.

OUR REAL RICHES

How important are your material possessions? Not as important as you might think. In the life of a committed Christian, material possessions should play a rather small role. In fact, when we become overly enamored with the things we own, we needlessly distance ourselves from the peace that God offers to those who place Him at the center of their lives.

Of course, we all need the basic necessities of life, but once we meet those needs for ourselves and for our families, the piling up of possessions creates more problems than it solves. Our real riches, of course, are not of this world. We are never really rich until we are rich in spirit.

Do you find yourself wrapped up in the concerns of the material world? If so, it's time to reorder your priorities by turning your thoughts and your prayers to more important matters. And, it's time to begin storing up riches that will endure throughout eternity: the spiritual kind.

MORE POWERFUL IDEAS ABOUT MATERIALISM

A society that pursues pleasure runs the risk of raising expectations ever higher, so that true contentment always lies tantalizingly out of reach.

Philip Yancey and Paul Brand

If you want to be truly happy, you won't find it on an endless quest for more stuff. You'll find it in receiving God's generosity and in passing that generosity along.

Bill Hybels

TODAY'S TIP FOR HANDLING TOUGH TIMES

The world wants you to believe that money and possessions can buy happiness. Don't believe it! Genuine happiness comes not from money, but from the things that money can't buy—starting, of course, with your relationship to God and His only begotten Son.

QUESTIONS TO CONSIDER

Do I genuinely understand that material possessions will not bring me lasting happiness?

_____

_____

Do I understand that my possessions are actually God's possessions, and do I use those possessions for His purposes?

_____

_____

Do my spending habits reflect the values that I hold most dear, and am I a faithful steward of my resources?

_____

_____

A PRAYER FOR TODAY

Heavenly Father, when I focus intently upon You, I am blessed. When I focus too intently on material possessions, I am troubled. Make my priorities pleasing to You, Father, and make me a worthy servant of Your Son. Amen

Day 26

DEFEATING
PROCRASTINATION

When you make a vow to God,
don't delay fulfilling it,
because He does not delight in fools.
Fulfill what you vow.
Ecclesiastes 5:4 Holman CSB

Not now becomes never.
Martin Luther

W hen tough times arrive, it's easy (and tempting) to avoid those hard-to-do tasks that you would prefer to avoid altogether. But the habit of procrastination takes a double toll: First, important work goes unfinished, and second, valuable energy is wasted in the process of putting off the things that remain undone.

God has created a world that punishes procrastinators and rewards men and women who "do it now." In other words, life doesn't procrastinate. Neither should you. So if you've been putting things off instead of getting things done, here are some things you can do:

1. Have a clear understanding of your short- and long-term goals, and set your priorities in accordance with those goals.

2. When faced with distasteful tasks, do them immediately, preferably first thing in the morning (even if the unpleasantness is a low-priority activity, go ahead and get it out of the way if it can be completed quickly). Dispatching distasteful tasks sooner rather than later will improve the quality of your day and prevent you from wasting untold amounts of energy in the process of fighting against yourself.

3. Avoid the trap of perfectionism. Be willing to do your best, and be satisfied with the results.

4. If you don't already own one, purchase a daily or weekly planning system that fits your needs. If used properly, a planning calendar is worth many times what you pay for it.

5. Start each work day with a clear written "to-do" list, ranked according to importance. At lunch time, take a moment to collect your thoughts, reexamine your list, and refocus your efforts on the most important things you wish to accomplish during the remainder of the day.

TODAY'S TIP FOR HANDLING TOUGH TIMES

The habit of procrastination is often rooted in the fear of failure, the fear of discomfort, or the fear of embarrassment. Your challenge is to confront these fears and defeat them.

MORE FROM GOD'S WORD ABOUT
PROCRASTINATION

If you do nothing in a difficult time, your strength is limited.

Proverbs 24:10 Holman CSB

Therefore, get your minds ready for action, being self-disciplined, and set your hope completely on the grace to be brought to you at the revelation of Jesus Christ.

1 Peter 1:13 Holman CSB

Lazy people's desire for sleep will kill them, because they refuse to work. All day long they wish for more, but good people give without holding back.

Proverbs 21:25-26 NKJV

Whatever you do, do it enthusiastically, as something done for the Lord and not for men.

Colossians 3:23 Holman CSB

Be strong and courageous, and do the work. Don't be afraid or discouraged, for the Lord God, my God, is with you. He won't leave you or forsake you.

1 Chronicles 28:20 Holman CSB

QUESTIONS TO CONSIDER

When something needs to be done, do I see the wisdom in doing it sooner rather than later?

_____

_____

Is the fear of failure holding me back?

_____

_____

When faced with an unpleasant job, do I act promptly, or do I increase my misery by procrastinating?

_____

_____

A PRAYER FOR TODAY

Dear Lord, when I am confronted with things that need to be done, give me the courage and the wisdom to do them now, not later. Amen

Day 27

IN TIMES OF UNCERTAINTY, CONSIDER THE POSSIBILITIES

For nothing will be impossible with God.
Luke 1:37 Holman CSB

Man's adversity is God's opportunity.
Matthew Henry

Are you afraid to ask God to do big things—or to make big changes—in your life? Is your faith threadbare and worn? If so, it's time to abandon your doubts and reclaim your faith in God's promises.

Ours is a God of infinite possibilities. But sometimes, because of limited faith and limited understanding, we wrongly assume that God cannot or will not intervene in the affairs of mankind. Such assumptions are simply wrong.

God's Holy Word makes it clear: absolutely nothing is impossible for the Lord. And since the Bible means what it says, you can be comforted in the knowledge that the Creator of the universe can do miraculous things in your own life and in the lives of your loved ones. Your challenge, as a believer, is to take God at His word, and to expect the miraculous.

Often God shuts a door in our face
so that he can open the door
through which he wants us to go.

—

Catherine Marshall

OPPORTUNITIES EVERYWHERE

As you look at the landscape of your life, do you see opportunities, possibilities, and blessings, or do you focus, instead, upon the more negative scenery? Do you spend more time counting your blessings or your misfortunes? If you've acquired the unfortunate habit of focusing too intently upon the negative aspects of life, then your spiritual vision is in need of correction.

Whether you realize it or not, opportunities are whirling around you like stars crossing the night sky: beautiful to observe, but too numerous to count. Yet you may be too concerned with the challenges of everyday living to notice those opportunities. That's why you should slow down occasionally, catch your breath, and focus your thoughts on two things: the talents God has given you and the opportunities that He has placed before you. God is leading you in the direction of those opportunities. Your task is to watch carefully, to pray fervently, and to act accordingly.

MORE POWERFUL IDEAS ABOUT POSSIBILITIES

Allow your dreams a place in your prayers and plans. God-given dreams can help you move into the future He is preparing for you.

Barbara Johnson

When God is involved, anything can happen. Be open and stay that way. God has a beautiful way of bringing good vibrations out of broken chords.

Charles Swindoll

TODAY'S TIP FOR HANDLING TOUGH TIMES

Focus on possibilities, not roadblocks. The road of life contains a number of potholes and stumbling blocks. Of course you will encounter them from time to time, and so will your family members. But, don't invest large quantities of your life focusing on past misfortunes. On the road of life, regret is a dead end.

QUESTIONS TO CONSIDER

Do I place my hopes in God?

_____

_____

Do I prayerfully seek to understand God's plans for my life?

_____

_____

Do I place limitations on myself, and do I place limitations on God's power to use me for His purposes?

_____

_____

A PRAYER FOR TODAY

Dear Lord, give me the courage to dream and the faithfulness to trust in Your perfect plan for my life. When I am worried, give me strength for today and hope for tomorrow. Today, Father, I will trust You and honor You with my thoughts, with my prayers, with my actions, and with my dreams. Amen

Day 28

IN TIMES OF
UNCERTAINTY,
GET BUSY

And whatever you do, do it heartily,
as to the Lord and not to men.
Colossians 3:23 NKJV

Let us not be content to wait and see
what will happen, but give us
the determination to make
the right things happen.
Peter Marshall

It isn't easy to overcome tough times—it takes hard work and lots of it. So if you're facing adversity of any kind, you can be sure that God has important work for you to do . . . but He won't make you do it. Since the days of Adam and Eve, God has allowed His children to make choices for themselves, and so it is with you. You can either dig in and work hard, or you can retreat to the couch, click on the TV, and hope things get better on their own.

The Bible instructs us that we can learn an important lesson from a surprising source: ants. Ants are among nature's most industrious creatures. They do their work without supervision, rumination, or hesitation. We should do likewise. When times are tough, we must summon the courage and determination to work ourselves out of trouble.

God has created a world in which diligence is rewarded and sloth is not. So whatever you choose to do, do it with commitment, excitement, and vigor. God didn't create you for a life of mediocrity or pain; He created you for far greater things. Reaching for greater things—and defeating tough times—usually requires work and lots of it, which is perfectly fine with God. After all, He knows that you're up to the task, and He still has big plans for you. Very big plans.

WHEREVER YOU ARE, WORK HARD

Wherever you find yourself, whatever your job description, do your work, and do it with all your heart. When you do, you will most certainly win the recognition of your peers. But more importantly, God will bless your efforts and use you in ways that only He can understand. So do your work with focus and dedication. And leave the rest up to God.

TODAY'S TIP FOR HANDLING TOUGH TIMES

Today, pick out one important obligation that you've been putting off. Then, take at least one specific step toward the completion of the task you've been avoiding. Even if you don't finish the job, you'll discover that it's easier to finish a job that you've already begun than to finish a job that you've never started.

MORE POWERFUL IDEAS ABOUT
THE NEED TO TAKE ACTION

Action springs not from thought, but from a readiness for responsibility.

Dietrich Bonhoeffer

God has lots of folks who intend to go to work for him "some day." What He needs is more people who are willing to work for Him this day.

Marie T. Freeman

Paul did one thing. Most of us dabble in forty things. Are you a doer or a dabbler?

Vance Havner

Logic will not change an emotion, but action will.

Zig Ziglar

It is by acts and not by ideas that people live.

Harry Emerson Fosdick

Pray as if it's all up to God, and work as if it's all up to you.

Anonymous

QUESTIONS TO CONSIDER

When I have work that needs to be done, do I usually try to finish the work as soon as possible, or do I put it off?

_____

_____

Do I believe that my testimony is more powerful when actions accompany my words?

_____

_____

Do I see the hypocrisy in saying one thing and doing another, and do I try my best to act in accordance with my beliefs?

_____

_____

A PRAYER FOR TODAY

Heavenly Father, when I am fearful, keep me mindful that You are my protector and my salvation. Give me strength, Lord, to face the challenges of this day as I gain my courage from You. Amen

Day 29

TIME FOR RENEWAL

I will give you a new heart
and put a new spirit within you.
Ezekiel 36:26 Holman CSB

God specializes in things fresh and firsthand.
His plans for you this year may outshine
those of the past. He's prepared to fill your days
with reasons to give Him praise.

Joni Eareckson Tada

On occasion, the demands of daily life can drain us of our strength and rob us of the joy that is rightfully ours in Christ. When we find ourselves tired, discouraged, or worse, there is a source from which we can draw the power needed to recharge our spiritual batteries. That source is God.

Is your spiritual battery running low? Is your energy on the wane? Are your emotions frayed? If so, it's time to turn your thoughts and your prayers to your Heavenly Father. When you do, He will provide for your needs, and He will restore your soul.

UNDERSTANDING DEPRESSION

Throughout our lives, all of us must endure personal losses that leave us struggling to find hope. The sadness that accompanies such losses is an inescapable fact of life—but in time, we move beyond our grief as the sadness runs its course and life returns to normal. Depression, however, is more than sadness . . . much more.

Depression is a physical and emotional condition that is, in almost all cases, treatable with medication and counseling. And it is not a disease to be taken lightly. Left untreated, depression presents real dangers to patients' physical health and to their emotional well-being.

If you're feeling blue, perhaps it's a logical response to the disappointments of everyday life. But if your feelings of sadness have lasted longer than you think they should—or if someone close to you fears that your sadness may have evolved into clinical depression—it's time to seek professional help.

Here are a few simple guidelines to consider as you make decisions about possible medical treatment:

1. If your feelings of sadness have resulted in persistent and prolonged changes in sleep patterns, or if you've experience a significant change in weight (either gain or loss), consult your physician.

2. If you have persistent urges toward self-destructive behavior, or if you feel as though you have lost the will to live, consult a professional counselor or physician immediately.

3. If someone you trust urges you to seek counseling, schedule a session with a professionally trained counselor to evaluate your condition.

4. If you are plagued by consistent, prolonged, severe feelings of hopelessness, consult a physician, a professional counselor, or your pastor.

God's Word has much to say about every aspect of your life, including your emotional health. And, when you face concerns of any sort—including symptoms of depression—remember that God is with you. Your Creator Father intends that His joy should become your joy. Yet sometimes, amid the inevitable hustle and bustle of life-here-on-earth, you may forfeit—albeit temporarily—God's joy as you wrestle with the challenges of daily living.

So, if you're feeling genuinely depressed, trust your medical doctor to do his or her part. Then, place your ultimate trust in your benevolent Heavenly Father. His healing touch, like His love, endures forever.

TODAY'S TIP FOR HANDLING TOUGH TIMES

God wants to give you peace, and He wants to renew your spirit. It's up to you to slow down and give Him a chance to do so.

QUESTIONS TO CONSIDER

Do I believe that God can make all things new—
including me?

_____

_____

Do I take time each day to be still and let God
give me perspective and direction?

_____

_____

Do I understand the importance of getting a good
night's sleep?

_____

_____

A PRAYER FOR TODAY

_Lord, You are my rock and my strength. When I grow
weary, let me turn my thoughts and my prayers to
You. When I am discouraged, restore my faith in You.
Let me always trust in Your promises, Lord, and let
me draw strength from those promises and from Your
unending love. Amen_

Day 30

A RENEWED SENSE OF PURPOSE

You will show me the path of life;
in Your presence is fullness of joy;
at Your right hand are pleasures forevermore.
Psalm 16:11 NKJV

God will make obstacles serve His purpose.

Mrs. Charles E. Cowman

I f you're experiencing tough times, you may be asking yourself "What does God want me to do next?" Perhaps you're pondering your future, uncertain of your plans, unsure of your next step. But even if you don't have a clear plan for the next step of your life's journey, you may rest assured that God does.

God has a plan for the universe, and He has a plan for you. He understands that plan as thoroughly and completely as He knows you. If you seek God's will earnestly and prayerfully, He will make His plans known to you in His own time and in His own way.

Do you sincerely want to discover God's purpose for your life? If so, you must first be willing to live in accordance with His commandments. You must also study God's Word and be watchful for His signs. Finally, you should open yourself up to the Creator every day—beginning with this one—and you must have faith that He will soon reveal His plans to you.

Perhaps your vision of God's purpose for your life has been clouded by a wish list that you have expected God to dutifully fulfill. Perhaps, you have fervently hoped that God would create a world that unfolds according to your wishes, not His. If so, you have probably experienced more disappointment than satisfaction and more frustration than peace. A better strategy is to conform your will to God's (and not to struggle vainly in an attempt to conform His will to yours).

Sometimes, God's plans and purposes may seem unmistakably clear to you. If so, push ahead. But other times, He may lead you through the wilderness before He directs you to the Promised Land. So be patient and keep seeking His will for your life. When you do, you'll be amazed at the marvelous things that an all-powerful, all-knowing God can do.

TODAY'S TIP FOR HANDLING TOUGH TIMES

Perhaps you're in a hurry to understand God's unfolding plan for your life. If so, remember that God operates according to a perfect timetable. That timetable is His, not yours. So be patient. God may have quite a few lessons to teach you before you are fully prepared to do His will and fulfill His purpose.

More from God's Word About Purpose

Whatever you do, do all to the glory of God.

1 Corinthians 10:31 NKJV

You're sons of Light, daughters of Day. We live under wide open skies and know where we stand. So let's not sleepwalk through life . . . .

1 Thessalonians 5:5-6 MSG

We look at this Son and see the God who cannot be seen. We look at this Son and see God's original purpose in everything created.

Colossians 1:15 MSG

To everything there is a season, a time for every purpose under heaven.

Ecclesiastes 3:1 NKJV

There is one thing I always do. Forgetting the past and straining toward what is ahead, I keep trying to reach the goal and get the prize for which God called me . . . .

Philippians 3:13–14 NCV

QUESTIONS TO CONSIDER

Do I understand the importance of discovering (or rediscovering, if necessary) God's unfolding purpose for my life?

_____

_____

Do I consult God on matters great and small?

_____

_____

Do I pray about my plans for the future, and do I remain open to the opportunities and challenges that God places before me.

_____

_____

A PRAYER FOR TODAY

Dear Lord, let Your purposes be my purposes. Let Your priorities be my priorities. Let Your will be my will. Let Your Word be my guide. And, let me grow in faith and in wisdom today and every day. Amen

Day 31

FOLLOW HIM

Then Jesus said to His disciples,
"If anyone wants to come with Me, he must deny
himself, take up his cross, and follow Me.
For whoever wants to save his life will lose it,
but whoever loses his life because of Me will find it."
Matthew 16:24-25 Holman CSB

You who suffer take heart.
Christ is the answer to sorrow.
Billy Graham

Jesus walks with you. Are you walking with Him seven days a week, and not just on Sunday mornings? Are you a seven-day-a-week Christian who carries your faith with you to work each day, or do you try to keep Jesus at a "safe" distance when you're not sitting in church? Hopefully, you understand the wisdom of walking with Christ all day every day.

Jesus loved you so much that He endured unspeakable humiliation and suffering for you. How will you respond to Christ's sacrifice? Will you take up His cross and follow Him—during good times and tough times—or will you choose another path? When you place your hopes squarely at the foot of the cross, when you place Jesus squarely at the center of your life, you will be blessed.

Do you seek to fulfill God's purpose for your life? Do you seek spiritual abundance? Would you like to partake in "the peace that passes all understanding"? Then follow Christ. Follow Him by picking up His cross today and every day that you live. When you do, you will quickly discover that Christ's love has the power to change everything, including you.

Your Eternal Journey

Eternal life is not an event that begins when you die. Eternal life begins when you invite Jesus into your heart right here on earth. So it's important to remember that God's plans for you are not limited to the ups and downs of everyday life. If you've allowed Jesus to reign over your heart, you've already begun your eternal journey.

Today, give praise to the Creator for His priceless gift, the gift of eternal life. And then, when you've offered Him your thanks and your praise, share His Good News with all who cross your path.

Today's Tip for Handling Tough Times

Following Christ is a matter of obedience. If you want to be a little more like Jesus . . . learn about His teachings, follow in His footsteps, and obey His commandments.

More from God's Word About
Following Christ

But whoever keeps His word, truly in him the love of God is perfected. This is how we know we are in Him: the one who says he remains in Him should walk just as He walked.

1 John 2:5-6 Holman CSB

We encouraged, comforted, and implored each one of you to walk worthy of God, who calls you into His own kingdom and glory.

1 Thessalonians 2:12 Holman CSB

The one who loves his life will lose it, and the one who hates his life in this world will keep it for eternal life. If anyone serves Me, he must follow Me. Where I am, there My servant also will be. If anyone serves Me, the Father will honor him.

John 12:25-26 Holman CSB

You did not choose Me, but I chose you. I appointed you that you should go out and produce fruit, and that your fruit should remain, so that whatever you ask the Father in My name, He will give you.

John 15:16 Holman CSB

QUESTIONS TO CONSIDER

Do I really believe that my relationship with
Jesus should be one of servant and Master. And I
am behaving like His servant

_____

_____

Am I attempting to follow in Christ's footsteps,
despite my imperfections?

_____

_____

Do I sense a joyful abundance that is mine when
I follow Christ?

_____

_____

A PRAYER FOR TODAY

*Dear Jesus, because I am Your disciple, I will trust
You, I will obey Your teachings, and I will share Your
Good News. You have given me life abundant and
life eternal, and I will follow You today and forever.
Amen*